ADDITIONAL BOOKS PUBLISHED BY MARIAN E. TURENNE

"All Through the Blood - Forgiven to Forgive"

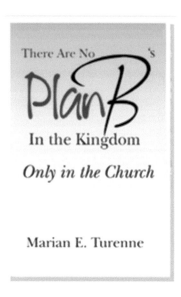

"There Are No Plan B's In the Kingdom - Only in the Church*"*

IN MEMORY OF:

Angela LaTease Bunn

Dedicated to my Family

Jason, Monica Justice and Mariah Bunn

Discussion Day Leads Excerpts taken from

"All Through the Blood – Forgiven to Forgive" (Published 2009)

Author's Photo – Terrence Adderley (www.terrenceadderley.com)

Cover Image - Godfrey W. Olive

'A Special Thank You'

Boston Public Library, Mattapan Branch

To the Administrator, adult computer lab, front desk and security staff.

Scripture Quotes Taken from The Holy Bible

KJV/NKJV/NIV/NLT/MSG/ES & TNTR Versions

All Quotes Appropriately Credited

To order additional copies of this book, contact:
Xlibris
1-888-795-4274
www.Xlibris.com
Orders@Xlibris.com

FORGIVEN TO FORGIVE

A Transparent Journey

—— DISCUSSION GUIDE ——
TO COMPLETE FORGIVENESS AND RECONCILIATION

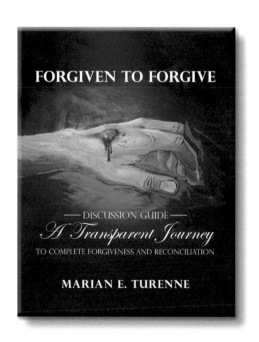

MARIAN E. TURENNE

FORGIVEN TO FORGIVE WAS WRITTEN TO
THE GLORY OF GOD AND FOR THE
ADVANCEMENT OF THE KINGDOM.
Marian E. Turenne

A SPECIAL
HONOR AND
TRIBUTE

This Discussion Guide is being dedicated IN HONOR and IN LOVING MEMORY of my daughter, Angela LaTease Bunn who loved me enough to challenge the call she saw on my life, even when it wasn't obvious to me. There will come a time in our lives when we will be required by God to step-up and challenge those we love, no matter how it's received.

Far too often we limit our 'Gifting's' to the familiar, and we do well, but God has a greater commission for us than we could ever imagine in His Kingdom. You ever experience times in your life when you felt like you should be doing something, but you just couldn't figure out what? I was at that point once and I remember crying out to the Lord…"FATHER, WHAT IS IT I'M SUPPOSE TO BE DOING?" This is how He answered.

On one occasion while trying to convince Angela, who was not only a beautiful young lady but was INGENOUSLY gifted by God, and a Creative/Thinker & Writer to let me edit some of her work, she got a *little* beside herself. Looking up from the computer, peering over the top of her glasses, and slightly raising her voice, with a 'ghetto attitude' said, "Mummy you need to STOP!" Never mind editing my work, God's got a book in you!" I looked at my daughter like she had three heads, and responded with an Rrrrrrr? *(That's the sound Scooby Doo my favorite cartoon character makes when something doesn't make sense to him).* Well, I never! …I was torn between throwing my shoe at Angy, responding with a flippant remark, or just ignoring her all together. Oh, but the wake-up call, the thing that God used to push me into place, yes, and *rock* my world, was an IQ Test I took on-line called *Tickle Test.* Taking it was lots of fun but most of all it was FREE! And yes, I absolutely believe God used it to get my attention.

The test results pointed out that the way I process information makes me a *Linguistic Architect.* Now keep in mind, even though taking the test was a lot of fun, thought provoking, and at times very difficult I never imagined the results would be so serious nor all that conclusive. What became crystal clear to me was that what God revealed to Angela to be true about me was verified through that test. It couldn't have been made any clearer. Here were the results: *"You are brilliant with language and words. You are also very skilled at understanding things on an abstract or conceptual level. When you combine those two skills you are bound to communicate or create something new and complex. This set of strengths (referred to as 'abstract reasoning,' meaning you have a flair for the intangible, intellectual, theoretical approach to life) allows you to understand math and science on a 'gut' level, even if the actual numerical math and science equations don't come easy. This gut-level understanding is typically enough to get you through without needing all of the details.* You would probably do well as a writer of some kind or an author whose job it is to get difficult concepts across skillfully." I wasn't the least bit moved by all the *brilliant, intangible, intellectual, theoretical* stuff…! It was the **"you would probably do well as a writer or some kind of an author part…"** I thought to myself… WHAT? At that very moment I began crying. Seconds later I gently heard Holy Spirit say…"DO YOU HEAR ME NOW?" That was a defining moment in my life and three years later, in 2009, I published my first book "ALL THROUGH THE BLOOD-FORGIVEN TO FORGIVE." Oh but it didn't end there, Angela then began challenging me with a, "Mummy, you need to write a Workbook to ATTB. People have to be taught and challenged through the forgiveness process." My daughter was relentless you all, and she didn't let me off the hook.

From the moment Angela could talk we knew she had a kind, attentive spirit. At 12 she gave her heart to the Lord and her tender-heartedness, creativity and faithfulness was put on full blast by Holy Spirit. If you needed a listening ear and encouraging counsel she was always available. If you were planning a Special Event and had no idea what to do, Angy would listen, envision how it could look, pull it together and then present it to you on a silver platter. She had the joy of serving under the Leadership of her Grandfather the Late Bishop Samuel L. Anderson at The United Emmanuel Holiness Church where she grew up. Dad always encouraged and provided training for Angela so she could minister her Gifting and Creativity to the Glory of God and the advancement of the Kingdom. During her 15yr residency in North Carolina she remained actively involved in ministry by sacrificially serving and using her gifting's to encourage, push and train others. Angela was a phenomenal simple to the point Bible teacher, liturgical dancer, and author. She was a well-loved Lead Childcare Teacher; Nanny and Administrator in the ministries where she served. She established a Ministry that was dear to her heart called 'LEGACY.'

In September of 2017, Angela returned home with plans to expand her ministry under new Leadership and of course with the same challenge for me on the tip of her tongue, "Mummy, have you started that Workbook yet?" But now she spoke in a, what are you waiting for tone.

Two months later on Saturday, November 4th she passed away suddenly. If it had not been for her challenge, love and encouragement ATTB would not have been published nor this Discussion Guide completed. I am so grateful to God for Angela's dedication, determination and her willingness to obey Him. More than anything I am so grateful she was 'my' daughter.

If you ever had the privilege of meeting, serving alongside or working with Angela, and you got to know her, I'm sure somewhere along the way she challenged, encouraged and pushed you as well to step out in Faith and put your gifting to work. Take my advice….GET BUSY!

FROM THE AUTHOR

Writing this Discussion Guide has been both a privilege and a challenge. Has anyone ever said, *"You haven't gotten over that yet?"* Or how about the infamous *"You need to stop, and move on!"* The most inconsiderate question is asked and advice given without offering a solution. My Goal is to provide a well-structured, challenging and supportive forum where fruitful conversations can be held as together Biblical Forgiveness is discovered. For the Believer there is a side of loving God that must be active in your life. John 14:21 (AMP) Jesus said, ***"The person who has My commandments and keeps them is the one who loves Me, and whoever loves Me will be loved by my Father, and I will love him and reveal Myself to him."*** On and on the Word exposes the benefits of our keeping the unconditional commands of God. Our Love for Christ and obedience to God's Word is a fundamental Act of our Spiritual Worship. For us, forgiveness is not optional, and a must in reconciling broken relationships.

To the Non-Believer who has been deeply wounded due to no fault of your own, I know, this journey sounds 'absolutely crazy'. You've even taken a, "I will never ever forgive them for what they've done to me" stance. "But trust me please"… If you're tired of the 'battle' you're in and really want to be free of all the emotional baggage you've carried around for so long, you're in the right place. And I want you to know that God loves you too!

My prayer is that you are willing to take the necessary time needed to push against the cultural complacency that's been perpetrated, and begin courageously meeting every challenge as it is presented. You've struggled; you're emotionally tired and disconnected and now you're enslaved to un-forgiveness. You've even wondered just how serious God is about this 'forgiveness thing.' To you it sounds crazy… But please, hold on…I have good news! First of all, God takes forgiveness **very** seriously which is why he sacrificed his only Son just for you. Some of you are thinking, "I just can't do this!" or like I thought, "I don't want to do this!"… Let me remind all that are Believers…YES YOU CAN! This is a step forward 'IN' Faith for you. Because Philippians 4:13 (NIV) declares, *"I can do all this through him who gives me strength"* means it is **possible.** This journey will be much tougher for some than for others, it will look, feel and sound impossible. But if you're *"willing"* to go 'through' to the end…you will experience freedom! God's principles at work, if followed and applied are beneficial to Believers and non-believers alike. He requires and responds to Faith that is visible, so let's get a steppin'.

I'm recommending this Journey be taken in a Family setting, Bible Study group; Sunday school class, Pastors & Leadership Training, Social or Book Club, and Men's & Women's Fellowship Group where everyone involved can go through the entire process together. At the beginning of each Discussion Day I share excerpts from my Book ATTB of my personal battles journeyed through to complete forgiveness as a lead into the challenges I'm confronting you with. Without a doubt, by the time you get to end of this Guide you will experience Christ's amazing love for you, the truth that He is the Son of the Living God, and that you too have been **FORGIVEN TO FORGIVE.**

Marian E. Turenne

WE'VE BEEN CREATED WITH PURPOSE

Each of us has been created by God with purpose. The cultural smugness in our society today that's crept into our churches and says 'oh don't worry, you're only human, God understands,' needs to be confronted and challenged. Un-forgiveness has created deep roots of resentment and hurt in the hearts of many. It's causing a hardness that's limiting their ability to stay confident while living in the present that we need to invest greater attention to dealing with. The Prophet Jeremiah teaches that God being like a Potter desires to form us like clay, soft and pliable in his hands.

The *Shofar* is being blown against the callousness that's been accepted while at the same time uncovering our reasoning and refusal to assume responsibility for personal choices. Spiritual inventory must be taken if we are to live up to our potential, while fulfilling our God given purpose. I unashamedly expose my harebrained experiences in order to instigate and set in motion the personal repositioning needed that goes beyond every traumatic experience, circumstance, or personal struggle and excuse. Whether you are the offended or the offender the challenge IS ON. The 'root' must be identified, dug up and exposed; the Biblical solution must be applied and the vicious cycle you're in must come to an end. WE HAVE PURPOSE PEOPLE! Wouldn't it be great if we could just forgive others and forget like God does for us?

All my life I was taught Jesus loved me and that God had a purpose and plan for me life. But it wasn't until I was in a 'personal relationship with Christ' that I knew there really was Hope, Help; and most of all there was Spiritual Healing for me. If you are willing to pursue your purpose and do what's right before God you too will come into the same truth.

My prayer is that if you're not already in a personal committed relationship with Christ Jesus as your 'Savior' that by the completion of your journey through this DOSCUSSION GUIDE you will be. Know this, Jesus loves and has purpose for you too. This is a Divine Intersection your about to enter and I encourage you to Stop, look and listen!

> *"Purpose is the foundation of vision. Vision is a manifestation of purpose. Purpose is what you were born to do!"*
>
> *The Late Dr. Myles Munroe*

INTRODUCTION

To successfully make it through to the end of this Discussion Guide you must be willing to invest the time necessary, while committing to being transparent and honest. You can't go through this halfheartedly. This journey requires a wholehearted effort on your part. You will be challenged to apply the Biblical Principles at work while uprooting your hurt, disappointment and fears. The greatest battle in the lives of most Believers is producing the fruit of Personal Holiness needed in a right relationship with Christ. We covet and fill positions in our churches; on our jobs, in our legislation and in our communities. We hold impressive titles and usurp authority over others but we don't allow the sanctifying Washing of God's Word to renew our minds. He alone has provided us through Holy Spirit the power needed to live progressively free, forgiven lives.

If you're not born-again yet but are willing and ready to expose the pain of your toxic behavior and relationships, the resentment, trauma and emotional despair you've lived through, and may have put others through, you too will move forward into progressive healing. Your willingness to apply the Biblical Principles enclosed, whether you initially understand them or not, are the key factors to moving forward. On your journey I pray you discover your need of a life changing relationship with the King of Kings and Lord of Lords, Jesus Christ Himself!

In your groups all the personal successes made should be celebrated, and joys shared. At times you might laugh at yourselves or with each other, or even cry together over dumb choices made. Shucks you might even think like I did, "WHAT A COMPLETE JERK I'VE BEEN.' But one thing is guaranteed, if you take the time needed to journey through to 'Forgiveness' you will reach a place of healing whether you are the offended or the offender. What's our focus here? The Love Christ demonstrated on that Cross just for you.

THIS IS AN 8 DAY JOURNEY!

ARE YOU READY FOR THE CHALLENGE?

CONTENTS

Introduction

DISCUSSION DAY ONE

WE MUST ID THE ROOT

WHAT'S THE ROOT OF YOUR PROBLEM?

Wounded	Demanding
Competitive	Anxious
Unreliable	Ungrateful
Hasty	Negligent
Bossy	Critical
Unteachable	Depressed
Patronizing	Retaliator
Double-minded	Self-centered
Boastful	Resistant
Fearful	Un-forgiving
Aggressive	Impolite
Prideful	Complainer
Disrespectful	Negative
Seeker	Thin Skinned
Arrogant	Gossiper
Deceitful	Envious
Player Hater	Compares
Argumentative	Nasty Spirited
Harsh	Easily Provoked
Pessimistic	**Takes Everything Personal**

When we are sick, the *symptoms* of our illness tend to show up way before the '*root*' is exposed.
We may face symptoms such as paralyzing anxiety, anger out of control, marriage
in distress, financial chaos, and much more. We lack peace and long for relief.
Susan Thomas

But if we confess our sins to him, he is faithful and just to forgive us our
*sins and to cleanse us from all wickedness. **John 1:9.** (NLT)*

THE CHALLENGE

'It's me O God' (excerpt from ATTB published in 2009)

My relationship with each of my parents was very different. Although I believe my mother really tried to love all of us the same, I always felt relationally at odds with her for most of my life never receiving the validation I needed. Please don't misunderstand me, my mother was a good woman, she took great care of her family, she taught me well and I learned some powerful life skills and lessons from her. But like some of you who have experienced strained parental relationships, my reality was that the bond just wasn't there. The stamina that was developed in my life and the affirmation I received came because of the relationship I had with my father. He and I were very close and next to Christ, he knew me best. Every day around our dinner table dad always challenged my siblings and I to become all God created and gifted us to be. He was a nurturer and a Legacy minded Man. As children my parents made sure we learned about Jesus at home first. During my Sunday school and VBS days I fell in love with Him. At age eight, he spoke to my heart comforting me during a time that I felt troubled and things had gotten real confusing for me concerning my mother. I clearly heard Jesus say, *"Marian, your mother doesn't know how to love you."*

At ten I played one of the main characters in a Sunday school Play entitled *"The Optimist and the Pessimist."* I had the role of the optimist, which along with my home teaching and training helped develop my perspective on life, for life. The lessons I learned from the Play so affected me that I vowed, at ten, to always try and see the glass *half full.* Writer Albert Schweitzer wrote that *"An optimist is a person who sees a green light everywhere; while a pessimist sees only the red stoplight...the truly wise person is color-blind."* We tend to measure the value of a person by his or her education, talents and skills but God defines his value of us by the condition of our hearts, and so should we. Never did I want to see life from the perspective of a pessimist. In my heart I purposed that no matter what, I would look for the best in any given situation and the very best in every individual unless otherwise proven wrong.

It became clear to me that God providentially positioned my dad to be a buffer between my mother and me. There always seemed to be this unspoken awareness he had regarding how I was feeling. But no matter how optimistic I tried to be at times I still struggled in my mind with our relationship. I desperately needed to share with someone what was going on, and how what I was experiencing was affecting me. Resentment occasionally rose up its ugly head and at times I found myself literally hating my mother. Sometimes even wishing she were dead. But I never ever disrespected her privately or publically, I knew way better than to do that. My heart attitude wasn't right in the sight of God. I just needed to know why what was happening was happening to me. Finally my dad and I had an opportunity to really talk. He didn't blow me off or try making me feel as if it were all my imagination. He didn't attempt to make it look like I was going through some kind of teenage thing. Nor did he seek making excuses for my mother. With all the compassion of Christ and his love for her dad shared situations and struggles that ma experienced in relationship with her mother which were caused by *'generational stuff'* that had taken 'root'. The 'root' of our problem was finally exposed. At that very moment I purposely chose to let go of the resentment and hatred that tried to take 'root' in my heart. All I can say is the clarity provided me an unspeakable confidence that I've forever walked in knowing that my mother's problem with me, wasn't because of me. And Just for the record I experienced many,

many enjoyable moments with her, but the question in the back of my mind was always …"I wonder how long this is going to last?"

Please understand me clearly; in no way was my relationship with my mother made any easier just because 'I' understood the 'root' of the problem. Neither did it lessen some of the disappointments I experienced at times. But it did cause me to make a conscious decision not to allow those generational 'roots' to take hold in me affecting my relationship with my children. After getting saved I chose to go into "*Christ management mode*" loving her in spite of what was happening. As awkward and difficult as it sometimes was, I chose to love and respect my mother in spite of, with a compassion and love that only came through my personal relationship with and growth IN Christ Jesus. But hear me, and hear me clearly, **there were times that the love and compassion I 'vowed' to live by were challenged.**

DOES ANYONE KNOW WHAT I'M TALING ABOUT???

Luke 6:27 (NIV)
Love for potential Enemies *27 "But to you who are listening I say: Love your enemies, do good to those who hate you*

OKAY LET'S GET REAL

"There is tremendous power in the act of forgiveness. Of course, forgiving is not always an easy thing to do". **Dr. Gary Thompson**

In order to expose the 'root' that's causing your hurt, your refusal to forgive and why, complete honesty, transparency and willingness to openly share is crucial at this point of the discussion. Getting to that 'root' involves dealing with what you can't see, caused by what you do see. Your self-disclosure will foster a deeper fellowship within the group. Without a willingness to be transparent, you cannot bear each other's burdens, comfort one another; encourage each other; push each other to forgive; care for one another nor weep or rejoice with each other. **ARE YOU READY?**

1. Are you Born-Again?   Yes _____ NO _____ Not Sure _____

2. Deep in your heart, do you really BELIEVE God LOVES and has FORGIVEN you?

    Yes _____ NO _____ Not Sure _____

3. Are you ready to admit, dig up, expose and discuss the 'ROOT' of your battle?

    Yes _____ NO _____ Not Sure _____

4. Are you PREPARED to begin the Forgiveness Challenge?

    Yes _____ NO _____ Not Sure _____

5. Are you WILLING to openly confess that you do have a forgiveness problem?

    Yes _____ NO _____

6. Have you been emotionally, physically, spiritually or psychologically WOUNDED?

    Yes _____ NO _____

7. Have you personally CONFRONTED or publically exposed your offender (s)?

    Yes _____ NO _____

8. WOULD you ever want to meet-up with that person again in life?

    Yes _____ NO _____ Not Sure _____

9. Whether you are the offended or the offender have you personally REPENTED?

    Yes _____ NO _____

10. What reason (s) have you used to RESIST forgiving another person?

_____

_____

11. Was there anyone you TRUSTED, confided in and discussed your hurt with?

Yes _____ NO _____

12. Did you feel SUPPORTED? Yes _____ NO _____

13. If so, after EXPOSING your hurt, use ONE word to describe how you felt emotionally.

_____

14. Were you COUNSELED? Yes _____ NO _____

15. Did you FOLLOW the counsel given? Yes _____ NO _____

16. Have you ever made a decision and later REGRETTED it? Yes _____ NO _____

17. Was anyone OFFENDED because of your decision? Yes _____ NO _____

18. Did you ASK forgiveness of that person? Yes _____ NO _____

19. Have you ever thrown or hosted a "PITY PARTY?" Yes _____ NO _____

20. From the list of "WHAT'S THE ROOT OF YOUR PROBLEM?" which ones best describes you? (Please be truthful)

_____   _____   _____

_____   _____   _____

_____   _____   _____

TAKE SOME TIME TO THINK THROUGH AND OPENLY DISCUSS YOUR ANSWERS

NOTES
Instead of Weakness, lay hold of Strength

_____

_____

_____

_____

_____

_____

_____

_____

_____

_____

_____

_____

_____

_____

_____

_____

_____

_____

_____

_____

"Father I've struggled through to this place in the process. Opening up has not been easy. Discussing where I am right now has been hard. You said that if I confessed 'my' sins, you'd be faithful and just to forgive me and clean me up from all unrighteousness. I confess me to you right now."

DISCUSSION DAY TWO

FORGIVENESS DOESN'T COME CHEAP

There is no such thing as cheap grace. Forgiveness always costs the person doing the forgiving. It was true for God and true for you and me. **Daniel R. Ledwith**

GOD'S UNENDING FAITHFULNESS

"To forgive is the highest, most beautiful form of Love.
In return, you will receive untold Peace and Happiness." **Robert Mull**

JUST FOR ME "And you too"

(Excerpt from ATTB published in 2009)

Author Daniel R. Ledwith wrote and I whole heartily agree: "For the Father to forgive us, it cost the life of His Son. God's grace did not come cheap. But just because Jesus bore the punishment for the sins of His people, it does not follow that there is no cost to us when we forgive someone."

In the Old Testament the Priests were required by God to offer up all day, every day burnt offerings which sacrificially and ceremonially cleansed the people from their sin. The High Priest on The Day of Atonement went through the Temple Veil into the Holy of Holies presenting himself a consecrated offering along with an unblemished animal. These were the sacrificial practices through which God provided forgiveness for the entire nation. But Christ, THE *Sacrificial Lamb of God*, once and for all through the shedding of His precious Blood paid the ultimate price for you and me, delivering us from the *penalty* of sin. Romans chapter 8:2 powerfully states our new position, *"For the law of the Spirit of life in Christ Jesus hath made me free from the law of sin and death."* Because Christ demonstrated his love for us at Calvary we're not required to bring an unblemished lamb or any other animal before the pastor and congregation to be slaughtered in order to be forgiven of our sin. We are simply commanded to repent, forsake and present ourselves as living sacrifices, holy and acceptable which is our reasonable service. Comprehending the sacrifice Christ made, His Deity and the redemptive power offered through His Blood, is foundational to our steadfast faith in Him.

When I think back on the process Israel went through just to be forgiven, I declare, if I had lived back in the day my tent would have been pitched right outside the temple gate to make sure I was first in line every day.

.

*God sent **Jesus** to redeem us from sin and death - He **paid off** our debt to death,*
*...**Christ** in His death on the cross had in view the payment **price**. **FB Daily Quotes***

"We know the recovery journey is filled with twists and turns. It isn't linear and there will be bumps in the road. Those bumps come in various forms. They may come as a thought that starts a spiral of negative self-talk and beating ourselves up. It may come in the form of an action, where we engage in some kind of behavior that we said we were not going to do." Alison Malee

THE FORGIVENESS TEST

Take your time, think the questions through and then complete this Forgiveness Test. At the end you will understand how important forgiveness is to your physical, mental and spiritual life. Let's see how well you understand what it means to **EARNESTLY FORGIVE.**

THINK FIRST AND IN COMPLETE HONESTY CIRCLE TRUE OR FALSE TO THE FOLLOWING QUESTIONS.

Questions:

T or F   1. Forgiveness is optional and is based totally on my feelings.

T or F   2. Forgiveness is all right to grant as long as the offender deserves it.

T or F   3. Forgiveness is honored by God.

T or F   4. Forgiveness involves everyone else but me to confess or make up.

T or F   5. Forgiveness is not a natural act of kindness and can be tough to do.

T or F   6. Forgiveness and reconciliation are the same.

T or F   7. Forgiveness is not Okaying or sanctioning what the person did.

T or F   8. Forgiveness lessens the illegal, bad or wrong that was done to you.

T or F   9. Forgiveness is letting the offender off the hook by granting a Pardon.

T or F   10. Forgiveness as hard as it is must be offered continuously.

Forgiveness IS NOT......

Forgiveness **IS NOT** forgetting. **It IS NOT** condoning or absolving. **NEITHER** is it pretending **NOR** something done for the sake of the offender. It is **NOT** a thing that we just do by a brutal act of the will. It **DOES NOT** entail a loss of identity or specialness or of face. **It DOES NOT** release the offenders from obligations they may or may not recognize.

An understanding of these things will go a long way towards helping people enter into the process of forgiveness. The action of forgiveness must take place honestly; we must go to the heart of the offense. You can't forgive if you don't deal with the issue. Nobody comes to this naturally, this is a learned practice."

Teaching By Dr. David Jeremiah

TEST ANSWERS

OPEN DISCUSSION TIME

LET'S CONSIDER WHAT THE BIBLE TEACHES

Note: Whether you agree or disagree, the Scriptures are
'CLEAR' on what God says about Forgiveness

1. **False.** Forgiveness is a required act of obedience to God. <u>Mark 11:25*</u> (NKJV) **Forgiveness and Prayer** 25 "And whenever you stand praying, if you have anything against anyone, forgive him, **that your Father in heaven may also forgive you your trespasses.**

2. **False.** None of us deserves to be forgiven yet God forgives us. <u>Luke 6:37</u> **(NIV) Judging Others.** 37 "Do not judge and you will not be judged." Do not condemn, and you will not be condemned. **Forgive, and you will be forgiven**. *

3. **True.** When we choose to honor God and live by His Word, we are rewarded. <u>Proverbs 25:21-22 </u>**(NIV) What About My Enemies?** 21If your enemy is hungry, give him food to eat; and if he is thirsty, give him water to drink. 22 In doing this, you will heap burning coals on his head, and the LORD **will reward you.***

4. **False**. It doesn't matter what others do. Forgiveness is a personal act that is chosen regardless of what other's do. <u>Colossians 3:13</u> **(NLT) When You Are Offended.** "Make allowance for each other's faults, and forgive anyone who offends you. **Remember, the Lord forgave you**, so you must forgive others*

5. **True.** Forgiveness is not a natural response. It takes the power of Holy Spirit in you to be kind to someone who has wronged you. <u>Romans 7:18-25 </u>**(NIV) The One That Delivers.** 18 For I know that good itself does not dwell in me, that is, in my sinful nature.[a] For I have the desire to do what is good, but I cannot carry it out. 19 For I do not do the good I want to do, but the evil I do not want to do-this I keep on doing. 20 Now if I do what I do not want to do, it is no longer I who do it, but it is sin living in me that does it. 21 So I find this law at work: Although I want to do good, evil is right there with me. 22 For in my inner being I delight in God's law; 23 but I see another law at work in me, waging war against the law of my mind and making me a prisoner of the law of sin at work within me. 24 What a wretched man I am! Who will rescue me from this body that is subject to death? 25 **Thanks be to God, who delivers me** through Jesus Christ our Lord! Another meaning for "deliver" is to equip for the fight.*

6. **False.** It takes only one person to forgive but it will take you and the other person to reconcile. God's heart is that we be reconciled to one another, but this isn't always possible if the other person won't try. <u>Psalm 133:1</u> **(NIV) The goodness in Unity.** 1 **How good and pleasant it is** when God's people live together in unity.*

7. **True.** Forgiveness is not saying that what the person did was OK. What they did was not OK, that is why you need to forgive. Luke 23:34 **(NLT) Jesus said, "Father, forgive them** for they don't know what they are doing." And the soldiers gambled for his clothes by throwing dice..*

8. **False.** What the person did to you may have been horrific, unprovoked, and ungodly.

Forgiving them does not take away from their wrong doing. But if you hold on to the offense and anger linked with the hurt, you will not be healed. Ephesians 4:20-28 **(NIV) Give No Foothold.** [20]That, however, is not the way of life you learned [21] when you heard about Christ and were taught in him in accordance with the truth that is in Jesus. [22] You were taught, with regard to your former way of life, to put off your old self, which is being corrupted by its deceitful desires; [23] to be made new in the attitude of your minds; [24] and to put on the new self, created to be like God in true righteousness and holiness. [25] Therefore each of you must put off falsehood and speak truthfully to your neighbor, for we are all members of one body. [26] "In your anger do not sin"[a]: **Do not let the sun go down while you are still angry,** [27] and do not give the devil a foothold. [28] Anyone who has been stealing must steal no longer, but must work, doing something useful with their own hands, that they may have something to share with those in need.*

9. **False.** Only God pardons or measures out vengeance. He is the final judge so take the person off the hook and leave him/her to Him. Romans 12:17-19* **(NKJV) You Make the Difference.** [17]Repay no one evil for evil. Have[a] regard for good things in the sight of all men. [18] If it is possible, **as much as depends on you, live peaceably with all men**. [19] Beloved, do not avenge yourselves, but *rather* give place to wrath; for it is written, **"Vengeance *is* Mine, I will repay,"** **says the Lord.**

10. **True.** No matter how many times you are offended, you are commanded to forgive. Luke 17:3-4 **(NIV) Take Heed.** [3] So watch yourselves. "If your brother or sister[a] sins against you, rebuke them; **and if they repent, forgive them**. [4] Even if they sin against you seven times in a day and seven times come back to you saying 'I repent,' you must forgive them."

"In life, we can't control circumstances and the way people treat us, but we can control how we respond to situations and others." Dr. Linda Mintle

WHAT'S YOUR FORGIVENESS SCORE?

According to scripture how many did you get CORRECT? _____

According to scripture how many did you get INCORRECT? _____

Has your mind been changed about what Forgiveness is? Yes _____ NO _____

As you proceed through the DISCUSSION GUIDE

keep in mind the areas that you scored least in.

NOTES
Instead of Falsehood, **seek the Truth**

_____
_____
_____
_____
_____
_____
_____
_____
_____
_____
_____
_____
_____
_____
_____
_____
_____
_____
_____
_____
_____
_____
_____
_____
_____

"Father God, Thank You for Holy Spirit who is guiding and leading me to the Truth of your Word regrading forgiveness. Help me Holy Spirit to stay focused so that my heart and mind will align with that of Christ Jesus. Thank you for the price Christ paid in my stead."

DISCUSSION DAY THREE

WHAT DID I DO?

"Sincere forgiveness isn't colored with expectations that the other person apologizes or change. Don't worry whether or not they finally understand you. Love them and release them."
Sara Paddison

*"All the ways of a man are clean in his own sight But the L*ORD *weighs the motives."*
Proverbs 16:2

SMACK DOWN

"The Buck Stopped at Me" (Excerpt from ATTB published in 2009)

WHAT DID I DO? Have you ever asked yourself that question? Well when I honestly looked back over my life I had to confess that there wasn't much I DIDN'T DO. As innocent as I tried to appear before man, in God's sight I was as guilty as all get-out.

At 19 I married, which was the craziest thing I ever did in life. The best experiences I had during that time were the births of my two children Angela and Jason. They were the source of my greatest Joy. Like most young couples we went through some very traumatic moments in our marriage. I'm not trying to be funny or anything but one of those 'moments' could have landed me in prison for life. Oh yeah…life. The collapse of our marriage may not have been my fault initially but the things I did to justify the hurt I suffered weren't right. I just chose not to acknowledge it. You know how we do…"Hurt people, hurt people." And because I had not learned how to deal with my hurts without hurting, it was on! Ultimately our marriage failed and we divorced. Of course my excuse was that my Ex was the problem. What I was doing was justifying the mess I was a part of. You ever been there? Listen, I'm not claiming to have experienced the same things you did, but I've been where a whole lot of you are right now. Most of you probably weren't as willful as I was either. Whenever necessary I 'unjustifiably justified' myself.

At 27 I gave my heart to the Lord and actively sought to find out God's Will for me. Our Bible Study Class began going through the Book of Romans and when we got to Chapter 2:1 it literally blew my mode of excuse making right out the water, *"Therefore you have no excuse or defense or justification, O man, whoever you are who judges and condemns another. For in posing as judge and passing sentence on another, you condemn yourself, because you who judge are habitually practicing the very same things [that you censure and denounce]."* KABOOM…I was exposed! Only God knew what was really at work in my heart. Those around me heard my side of the story and at times I purposely embellished the facts for the sake of drawing support to further my own agenda. Yup, I LIED. Now however, I had to examine my intentions and my motives in light of God's Word. The Holiness of God and Sanctification, which is His Will for every Born-Again Believer, is a real work 'in progress.' The motives of our hearts are openly exposed and put on display for correction. One of the attributes in God's requirement of us living Holy is spiritual integrity. For those who are not yet Born-Again integrity a crucial characteristic needed in our society today when dealing with family, friends, and co-workers. There's no greater compliment than to be recognized as a person of integrity.

My church friends and I use to exchange relationship war stories but we never challenged each other's personal responsibility. I'm not sure why but as far as I was concerned that was A-Okay with me. No one asked, and I wasn't telling. I don't know about any of them but I had the starring role in my comedy of errors. *(Our silence automatically excused and exonerated any responsibility whatsoever we may have had individually).* They seemed to be amused at the crazy things I confessed to asking God for regarding my Ex, and I had the nerve to label them 'prayer requests.' Requests that were not funny, but no one said a thing, so we all laughed. Even though I wasn't being challenged by them Holy Spirit in my private time was calling my mess up on the rug. Ultimately their agreeing and sympathizing with me didn't matter. God had the final Word, in His Word. During that time I was also being counseled by my pastor who said, "Marian, all you have to be is 'willing' to allow God, through Holy Spirit to begin working 'IN' you. With permission He will direct your path according to God's Word, purposes and plan concerning you." I thought…I only have to be *willing*? All I needed to do was surrender you all! If you're seeking or receiving counsel make sure it's founded on The Word. The danger in being counseled incorrectly is that it can cause you to be dangerously off track and out of the Will of God. My pastor provided wise Godly, not friendly counsel. Gradually my perspective began to change as I willingly stepped out of my 'feelings' and gave into Holy Spirit's leading.

Moving beyond your emotions and opinions while refusing to allow bad experiences to govern your outcome is absolutely necessary. I read a devotional through Godspeaks.com which stated, *"God gave us our feelings and emotions. They're a gift that enables us to experience life in full color. A wedding, a funeral, a ballet recital…what would these events be like without emotions?"* You and I both know nothing close to what they could be. *"But as important as our feelings are, they need to be kept in their proper perspective. They are there to respond to reality, not to determine it. Oftentimes, our feelings cross this line in our hearts, and we allow the way we happen to feel to shape our perception of truth."*

God foreknew exactly when I would surrender my heart and life to Christ. And with all His foreknowledge He did not re-write the pages of scripture to accommodate me. Because He loves us, everything in our lives must come subject to His *Perfect* Will, which is the principal of the Kingdom. When we receive Christ we lay down our Rights and Will and everything about us over time begins to reflect and represent Him. In John 14:15 when Christ said, ***"If you love me keep my commandments"*** was never meant to be a suggestion; but a directive.

To those who have been willfully abused, and wounded beyond comprehension and you emphatically want to know, "What Did I Do?" The reality of your offender and those who continue to illegally and immorally abuse and offend others has been exposed in God's Word. What caused the offence may or may not have had anything to do directly with you. The violation began in the heart of the offender and The Word of God is clear about the why. Ephesians 4 states it's because they live and walk in, the self-importance of their minds, [18] ***having their understanding darkened, being alienated from the life of God, because of the ignorance that is in them, because of the blindness of their heart; 19 who, being unable to feel, have given themselves over to filthiness, to work all impurity with pleasure.*** That is who they are, and why they do what they do. But The Word does not let us off the hook just because we are aware of their condition (because in the past some of us lived just like them) and are now quick to declare them un-forgiven. We are commanded to live differently, so we don't take our cues from the world, our family or friends regarding this issue either, but from the Word alone. Ephesians also declares to us ***"to let all bitterness, wrath, anger, clamor, and evil speaking be put away from us, with all malice. And be kind to one another; tenderhearted, forgiving one another, even as God in Christ forgave us."*** That calls for a renewing in the spirit of our minds, and a putting on of the new self, created after the likeness of Christ in true righteousness and holiness. Christian Author Lewis B. Smedes said, "To forgive is to set a prisoner free and discover that the prisoner was you." The burden literally falls in the lap of the offended to forgive! God requiring 'us' to forgive our offenders doesn't make any sense, but the Choice is still yours to declare "THE BUCK STOPS AT ME!"

Holiness is more than a Doctrinal Teaching, an Article in our 'Mission Statements,' our Bylaws or a simple Church cliché; it is the perfect standard of God. It is the required lifestyle of every Born-Again Believer.

THE FOLLOWING QUESTIONS WERE TAKEN FROM THE EXCERPT

"The Buck Stopped at Me"

- When I asked 'WHAT DID I DO? For me it was an act of self-defense. But when I took an honest look back over my life I had to admit that there wasn't much **I didn't do**. What personal experiences came to mind as you read my confession? **Share**

_____

_____

_____

- The things I had the nerve to ask God for regarding my Ex, labeling them "Prayer Requests" really reflected my unwillingness to forgive him and weren't funny at all. Those around never challenged me. Have you been challenged by anyone regarding your unwillingness to forgive or the crazy things you may have said or done? **Share**

_____

_____

_____

- To those who have been willfully abused and wounded due to no fault of your own but still want to know, "What Did I Do?" How helpful was Ephesians 4 in clarifying the '**Why**' people do what they do? **Share**

_____

_____

_____

- Based on all that has been shared and discussed just how important has accountability and the need to be transparent become to you? **Share**

_____

_____

_____

Overcome Evil with **Good**

_____

_____

_____

_____

_____

_____

_____

_____

_____

_____

_____

_____

_____

_____

_____

_____

_____

_____

_____

_____

_____

_____

"Thank you Jesus for being so loving towards me even when I refused at times to love others. Thank you for taking me off center stage of my own life and beckoning me to follow you instead. Your Word holds true no matter what." Amen

DISCUSSION DAY FOUR

IT'S NOT EASY TO FORGIVE THOSE WHO OFFEND ME

Christ, by permission of his Father willingly became a sin substitute for you,
but are you just as willing to let Him be the same substitute for the individual(s)
who wounded you? That is not always easy. **(Author Unknown)**

*If I could speak all the languages of earth and of angels, but didn't love others, I would
only be a noisy gong or a clanging cymbal. If I had the gift of prophecy, and if I understood
all of God's secret plans and possessed all knowledge, and if I had such faith that I could
move mountains, but didn't love others, I would be nothing.* **1 Corinthians 13:1013 NLT**

HELP!

"A Red letter Day" (Excerpt from ATTB published in 2009)

(Just for the record, **A Red Letter Day** for me is defined as hearing directly from God's Word)

The movie *Forest Gump* was one of my all-time favorites! In it Tom Hanks played the character short of a few screws named Forest. Throughout the entire movie he made the most profound statement which he preceded with "Mama Always said." Over and over again he repeated one particular line that became my favorite catchphrase…"Mama always said, Stupid Is, as Stupid Does!" Proverbs 12:1 defines the word stupid as a person who refuses Wise Counsel. At one time in my life my name was the full blown definition of the word stupid. If you had looked it up in the dictionary my picture would have been right next to the definition.

In ATTB I shared the chain of events in my life as a witness to and picture of what stupid really looked like in motion. To those of you who find or have found yourselves in similar circumstances please heed the warnings! **CAUTION!**…a red light is still a red light no matter what corner it's posted on! Because of all the things I allowed myself to get caught-up in prior to getting saved, and hear me clearly; these were situations I allowed, so the consequences I suffered were due to my own stupidity. It is not God's will for us to go through the stuff we suffer, but when we become Believers He in his Sovereignty uses our bad choices and experiences to position us where he purposed for us to be from the beginning of time. Today I have complete confidence in God's infinite Wisdom, absolute Providence and Sovereignty.

As a parent I positioned myself as my children's primary care provider when it came to teaching and exposing them to life. It wasn't left up to their day care, public school or Sunday school teachers. Like my parents taught me, I taught them that taking personal responsibility is a must. That's why I couldn't have escaped taking blame for all I did if I tried. Choices made whether good or bad within our willpower, not forced upon us of course, are our doing not anyone else's. So whenever I decided to do wrong the consequences of my choices were carefully considered before I made my move. So the buck literally stopped at me.

As a Believer, even though I knew the Buck stopped at me, and I was really *'trying'* to surrender 'everything' to God, in the back of my mind I still question, "Why God do I have to be the one?" Because I wasn't willing to *totally* let go I found myself battling un-forgiveness unnecessarily. At times just the mention of my Ex's name pissed me off (I no longer use that word). What I was doing on my terms was extending "partial forgiveness", which is not forgiveness at all. Blame was still being laid at his feet that I wasn't ready to declare him forgiven of just yet. Look, to be perfectly honest as far as I was concerned he was in 'prison' with no parole in sight.

Something had to break because the more I began falling in Love with Jesus the deeper I absolutely knew in my heart harboring un-forgiveness hindered my growth and relationship with Him. There were times I knelt to pray or was in Bible study and Holy Spirit would bring him to mind. Like a spoiled child wanting their own way I'd get off my knees and sit down, or close my Bible and wait until the conviction passed. My 'unwillingness' nearly caused me to stumble over the Cross instead of kneeling there for healing and forgiveness. I absolutely knew that having a bad conscience was a violation of God's Word, so I needed to surrender and allow Holy Spirit to begin sanctifying my heart, and quickly. I dragged my feet because I felt like if I forgave the rascal it would be like letting him off the hook, which I thought was totally unfair to me. Because God deals only with what's true and not with what's fair He carried me back to Calvary reminding me of the price Christ' paid on my behalf so that I would be taken off the hook and forgiven. I really wanted to be able to see my Ex through the Cross which represents Christs Love and Compassion. But pay close attention to what's about to follow, you'll see yourself somewhere in the mix. Mind you, Forgiveness is a spiritual act involving a change of your perspective based on who you are now IN relationship with God through Christ Jesus. Ultimately we have to totally trust in His grace to achieve it by surrendering to His Lordship. What I finally understood was that 'to know, is to do', and we do things, by doing not by just talking. Talk really is cheap! But this is how really hard I made forgiving my Ex to be.

Even with all the truth that I was being taught, the Love God was pouring into my life and the power and ministry of Holy Spirit being evidenced around me, I still *'toyed'* with the **wee** possibility that maybe just maybe God was going to give me *'special'* consideration. Don't laugh! The enemy of my soul was attempting to have 'a field day' but I was trying to do what Paul encouraged us to do in the last part of Ephesians 4:26-27, "resist giving the enemy a foothold in your life." I knew it was God's Will that me Ex be saved but in my selfishness I focused only on me. Imagine the level of self-righteousness I was working in.

There's an Evangelistic Track which demonstrated the state I was *emotionally and spiritually* in better than any illustration I could ever use. It's called *My Heart, Christ's Home.* It's a picture of the human heart shaped like a house. Each room represented the different struggles and sins needing to be repented of consequently allowing the progressive cleaning up of my heart/mind and spirit. The concept demonstrates the need we have to *voluntarily* and *willingly* give up our sin. Some rooms I quickly surrendered handing over the keys giving Holy Spirit complete access and authority to go in and cleanout my mess. However, the room labeled 'ex-husband'; I nailed and super glued shut, blocked off with a bolder and hung a huge **'DON'T BOTHER TO DISTURB'** sign on it. If forgiving him only meant letting go so that I could be free, I might would have done that. But Oh No, forgiving him meant that I would have to love and pardon the rascal which I totally enjoyed not doing. But in the midst of all Holy Spirit was accomplishing in my heart one day a Life Lesson my dad taught, and considered an important principle came to mind. Dad said, "No matter the situation Marian, you always be the better person, be the example!" Listen you all putting that into practice was a *'real'* challenge, and to be honest I didn't want to always be the better person. And to be perfectly honest, there were times when I wasn't. In the back of my mind I used to wonder, why, why do I have to always be the better person? **WARNING!** Do not allow yourself to get drawn into the land of "WHY" because it has a tendency to take you far away from God's Will. He wants you to learn to trust him in the 'why.' The Word declares that we are now positioned in His Righteousness, justified children of God, in Christ. Daily we are to develop a Christ-like mindset all while demonstrating God's Love towards us. We are peacemakers and are to take the position of the mature ones. Besides I was also taught that whatever enemy I didn't deal with in life, my children would have to face. So for me, finally trusting God by Faith and ceasing from trying to do things my way transformed my entire life. (Faith is not only how we receive salvation but it is how we learn to live moment by moment, day by day). My getting to that place of Godly forgiveness was crucial. Un-forgiveness was not part of the Legacy I cared to leave my children or my grand-children. But because of all I had harbored in my heart forgiveness became achingly difficult to grant. No Lie. I was stuck in a place referred to as 'moderate forgiveness competency,' where I had some serious work to do on becoming less trapped by my past resentments. Come on you know what I'm talking about! But I thank God he allows us a Grace Period of time to get it right.

Holy Spirit can do a definite work in your heart that will, if allowed, transform your perspective. Growing-up in Christ I've learned to deal with every difficult relationship by applying the "you be the better person" principle. All I have to tell you is that *willful or fabricated ignorance* does not change the heart of God.

In my Daily Devotional time I would ask Holy Spirit to lead me to a scripture. Two things were made absolutely clear by doing that. 1. There was never a Book/Chapter or Verse that was not there, and 2. God would speak directly to me through the Word I was led to read. One day Holy Spirit led me to read Matthew 5:43-. When I found the chapter and verse I began reading. God was expressly speaking to my heart but the more I read the less I wanted to read. I was like…HUH

[43] Ye have heard that it hath been said; Thou shalt love thy neighbor, and hate thine enemy… OKAY. [44] But I say unto you, Love your enemies….HUH? Bless them that curse you….do good to them that hate you….WHAT? **And** pray for them which despitefully use you and persecute you…. PRAY FOR THEM? [45] That ye may be the children of your Father which is in heaven, **OMG**oodness!

Even though I was convicted I still had the nerve to ask God, "Father I have to **pray** for the rascal too?" Every time my Bible fell open to Matthew 5:43-45a the Lord would remind me in a still small voice, "Yup and you have to pray for the rascal too!"

During that same time Dr. Charles Stanley, one of my favorite radio pastors, did a teaching on *Un-forgiveness*. He taught that, *"When we allow a bitter spirit to lodge in our souls, it grows and festers; it becomes both painful and destructive."* This in addition to what I was already being taught really catapulted and helped in progressively transforming my life. I was in need of a genuine relationship repair.

It was evident and becoming super clear by what I was witnessing around me that un-forgiveness was the link tied at the toxic 'root' of many with physical, emotional, psychological, and spiritual problems. That's not how I wanted to live, and was learning that Forgiveness was the only way to break that tie and becoming FREE. When Apostle Paul wrote in Ephesians 4:31, 32 *"Let all bitterness, wrath, anger, clamor, and evil speaking be put away from you, with all malice, and be kind one to another, tenderhearted, forgiving one another, even as God in Christ forgave you,"* he wasn't making a suggestion. It was, and still is God's Will for us. Paul described the ugly manifestations of the "spirit of un-forgiveness." That spirit goes way beyond a temporary unwillingness to forgive the period between the time a person gets hurt, and the time she or he forgives the one who hurt them. A spirit of un-forgiveness develops when the one who got hurt chooses to remain in that state. People, who cultivate this, often are referred to as *nasty spirited*, and generally say stuff like, *"I just don't think I could ever forgive that."* Have you ever made that statement when you felt mistreated in such an unjust, unfair, harmful way? I'm sure you have, but if the truth be told it's not that you couldn't forgive, you just simply wouldn't. Oh Yeah, at one time in my life that was me in **'LIVING COLOR'**. Like all decisions in life made, un-forgiveness is a choice. It's made with your will-and it's a devastatingly bad choice, not only for the relationship, not only for the cause of Christ, but also for the one who refuses to forgive."

> *"When you hold resentment toward another, you are bound to that person or condition by an emotional link that is stronger than steel. Forgiveness is the only way to dissolve that link and get free."* **Catherine Ponder**

OPEN DISCUSSION TIME!

THE FOLLOWING QUESTIONS WERE CREATED FROM THE EXCERPT 'RED LETTER DAY'

KEEP IT HONEST AND TRANSPARENT

1. Have you recognized times in your life when instead of yielding to do what was right (whether you were the offended of the offender) you became 'Self-Righteous'?

Yes _____ No _____

2. If you are the offended, do you believe God is fair in commanding 'you' to forgive your offender?

Yes _____ No _____

3. Have you ever tried to get even, seek revenge, or retaliate against those who hurt you?

Yes _____ No _____

4. Do you have a 'Repay or Hit' Check list created?   Yes _____ No _____

5. If so how do you justify your motives? _____

_____

6. Are there any areas of un-forgiveness in your heart that you've blocked off with **"Do not bother to disturb"** signs?

Yes _____ No _____

7. Have you found comfort in holding onto un-forgiveness or grudges?

Yes _____ No _____

8. Has anyone ever referred to you as nasty spirited?   Yes _____ No _____

9. Do you believe un-forgiveness is a Choice or a right? Choice _____ Right _____

10. Are you DEALING with hurt from people who are still around you?

Yes _____ No _____

11. ☑The word(s) that bests describes the stage of un-forgiveness you're in right now? **Strong** (Trying to Stay Positive) _____ **Impaired** (Have major work to do) _____ In the **Danger Zone** (I need serious help and counseling) _____

12. Do you believe un-forgiveness can have toxic negative effects impairing your emotional, physical, spiritual and psychological health? Yes_____ No _____

13. Do you believe there's a need for real relationship repair after an offense takes place or it doesn't matter to you?

Yes_____ No _____ Doesn't Matter_____

14. When Apostle Paul spoke of bitterness, wrath, anger, chaos, and evil speaking, was he DESCRIBING the state you're in?

Yes _____ No _____

15. Do you understand how holding resentment towards another can literally keep you emotionally tied and bound to them?

Yes _____ No _____

16. Do you or do you know of anyeone who always manages to offend in action, word or deed?

Yes _____ No _____

17. Have you ever witnessed your offenses ending up being a blessing in someone else's life?

Yes _____ No _____

18. Share:

_____

_____

_____

_____

19. After reading the scripture portion of my story below where I was being required by God to change, what would your challenge have been?

Let's hear what you're honestly thinking

43 Ye have heard that it hath been said; Thou shalt love thy neighbor, and hate thine enemy 44 But I say unto you, Love your enemies, bless them that curse you....do good to them that hate you And pray for them which despitefully use you and persecute you.... 45 That ye may be the children of your Father which is in heaven... **Matthew 5:43**

Falling In Love with Jesus
Jonathan Butler

Falling in love with Jesus
Falling in love with Jesus
Falling in love with Jesus
was the best thing I ever, ever done

In his arms I feel protected
in his arms never disconnected
In his arms I feel protected
There's no place I'd rather, rather be

NOTES
Defeat Fear with **Faith**

"Father, by Faith I'm getting better at learning how to forgive, and from the depths of my heart, I say Thank You for the Love I'm experiencing. Thank you Jesus"

DISCUSSION DAY FIVE

WHY IS GOD SO BENT ON MY FORGIVING OTHERS?

SO WHAT'S LOVE GOT TO DO WITH IT?

"This is our reality: The infinite love of God. Whatever your earthly family or friends aren't, you have a Father in heaven who loves you immensely." **Pastor James MacDonald**

"Therefore, as God's chosen people, holy and dearly loved, clothe yourselves with compassion, kindness, humility, gentleness and patience. [13] Bear with each other and forgive one another if any of you has a grievance against someone. Forgive as the Lord forgave you " **Colossians 3:12-13**

TOGETHER WE ARE GOING

TO **D**ISSECT, **D**ISCUSS AND **D**ETERMINE

HOW MATTHEW 6:14, 15 APPLIES

Matthew **6:14, 15 (NIV)** *"For if you forgive other people when they sin against you your heavenly Father will also forgive you. But if you do not forgive others their sins, your Father will not forgive your sins"*

IF I DO NOT FORGIVE OTHERS, DOES THAT MEAN MY SINS ARE NOT FORGIVEN?

IT'S ON!

LET'S TAKE A LOOK AT 'WHY' GOD IS SO BENT ON OUR FORGIVING OTHERS

Matthew 6 does not teach that our eternal destiny is based on our forgiving other people; however, it does teach that our relationship with God will be damaged if we refuse to pardon those who have offended us. The Bible is clear that God pardons sin by His grace based on Christ's work on the cross alone, not on man's actions. Our right standing before Him is established on one thing only - the finished work of Christ (John 3:16; 1 John 2:2; 1 John 4:10). The penalty for the sin that is rightly ours was paid by Christ, and we obtain it by grace through faith, not by any righteous deeds of our own (Ephesians 2:8-9). No one will be able to stand before God demanding that his sins be forgotten simply because he has forgiven others. Only when we are born again and given a new life through God's Spirit by faith in Christ Jesus are our sins forgiven. Therefore, Jesus is not referring to God's initial act of forgiveness (reconciliation) that we experienced when we first believed the Gospel. What He is referring to is the day-to-day cleansing we obtain when we confess our sins in order to restore fellowship with our heavenly Father—the fellowship which is interrupted by the daily tarnishing of sin that affects us all. This is not the wholesale cleansing from sin that comes with salvation by grace through faith, but is more like the foot-washing Jesus describes in John 13:10. The "whole body is clean," He told the disciples, but their feet were dirty from their walking in the world. Forgiveness in this sense is what God threatens to withhold from Christians who refuse to forgive others.

In Matthew 6 Jesus is teaching disciples how to pray and in doing so outlines how we are restored into intimacy with God whenever we have displeased Him. In fact, Jesus instructs us to build into our prayers a request for God to forgive us in the same way that we have forgiven others who have harmed us (Matthew 6:12). If there are those we have not forgiven when we ourselves pray for forgiveness, then practically speaking we are asking God not to restore a right relationship with us after we sin. To emphasize the importance of restoring broken relationships with our brothers and sisters, Jesus states that asking for God's forgiveness for one's own sins, all the while withholding forgiveness from someone else, is not only bizarre but hypocritical. We cannot possibly walk with God in true fellowship if we refuse to forgive. To be sure, an unforgiving spirit is a serious sin and should be confessed to God. If we have un-forgiveness in our hearts against someone else, then we are acting in a way that is not pleasing to God, making our prayers and a proper living relationship with Him difficult. God will not hear our prayers unless we also show ourselves ready to grant forgiveness

A second biblically plausible interpretation of Matthew 6:14-15 is that it is saying anyone who refuses to forgive others is demonstrating that he has not truly received Christ's forgiveness himself. Any sin committed against us, no matter how terrible, is trivial in comparison to our sins against God. If God has forgiven us of so much, how could we refuse to forgive others of so "little"? Matthew 6:14-15, according to this view, proclaims that anyone who harbors un-forgiveness against others has not truly experienced God's forgiveness. Both interpretations strongly deny that salvation is dependent on our forgiving others. Whether Matthew 6:14-15 is speaking of "relational forgiveness," or whether it is a declaration that un-forgiveness is the mark of an unbeliever, the core truth is the same. We should forgive others because God, through Christ, has forgiven us. It is wrong for someone who has truly experienced God's forgiveness to refuse to grant forgiveness to others. How can Christians make *real* forgiveness an ongoing, practical part of everyday life, not just a popular spiritual cliché? Come on, Sin affects us!   Gotguestions.com

C.S. Lewis said, "To be a Christian means to forgive the inexcusable,
because God has forgiven "THE INEXCUSABLE IN YOU."

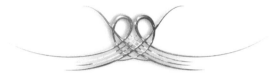

THIS IS A LITTLE BIT OF WHAT LOVE HAS TO DO WITH IT:

John 3:16 **For God so loved the world** that He gave His only begotten Son, that whoever believes in Him should not perish but have everlasting life.

I John 3:1 **How great is the love the Father has lavished on us**, that we should be called the children of God"

1 John 4:10 **In this is love, not that we loved God, but that He loved us** and sent His Son *to be* the propitiation for our sins.

I Cor. 13:4-7 **Love is patient, love is kind. It does not envy, it does not boast it is not proud**. It is not rude, it is not self-seeking, it is not easily angered, and it **keeps no record of wrongs.** Love does not delight in evil but rejoices with the truth. It always protects, always trusts, always hopes, and always perseveres. Love never fails…

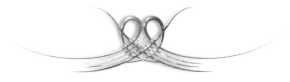

FORGIVENESS

Fill in the acrostic with words that you believe apply to **Forgiveness**.

Forgiveness *is the key that unlocks the door of resentment and the handcuffs of hatred. It is a power that breaks the chains of bitterness and the shackles of selfishness."* **Corrie ten Boon**

F

O

R

G

I

V

E

N

E

S

S

OPEN DISCUSSION TIME

NOTES
Instead of Ignorance, **choose Knowledge**

_____

_____

_____

_____

_____

_____

_____

_____

_____

_____

_____

_____

_____

_____

_____

_____

_____

_____

_____

"Father you have bought me to a place of real self-examination. It has not been comfortable or easy but it's only because I have read and am beginning to understand the Love you have towards me. I've learned that you are an "Unchanging God" and I have come to accept that truth."

DISCUSSION DAY SIX

INTENTIONAL

'I'M SORRY'...
'PLEASE,
FORGIVE ME'?

Creating an intentional life requires that we stop responding by emotions and start walking in truth.
Angela Craig

Figure out what will please Christ, and then do it. **Ephesians 5:10 (MES)**

I CAME TO GRIPS WITH ME

Be Careful (Excerpt from ATTB published in 2009)

Proverbs 3:5, 6 says *'Trust in the Lord with all your heart and lean not to your own understanding; in all your ways acknowledge him, and he will direct your path.'* The Word says in all your ways, which is not a selective acknowledgement either; it means just what it declares, in ALL your ways. Even in what you consider to be the little things, the Lord will direct your paths. This for some has become far easier said than done. You know how we are. We make things happen for ourselves, and then act like God had everything to do with it. When in all actuality we never even bothered to seek His counsel. If you're going to serve Him in Spirit and in Truth you are being required to give up your will for His Will. And when you practice asking God first and waiting on his answer before making a final decision, it decreases the worry and increases your confidence, faith and contentment. Listen, at first it was my inclination to try and do things my way too. I'd approach God with my agenda in hand trying to do new things my old way. You know how we do it…'my Will Father not yours be done.' But it never worked. The truth was and still is that if I need the 'know how' for what I'm about to do, all's I have to do is go straight to Him first. It was at that point when I came to grips with 'me' that things began to get a lot easier. Next time, so that you won't keep spinning your wheels like I did unnecessarily, pray and ask God to include you in His Plan, listen for his counsel, and then follow his lead.

Remember when we were kids and we got caught or blamed for doing something wrong? What was the very first thing we were made to say? …YUP, you got it, "I'm Sorry." In some cases we were made to say it whether we actually did what we were being blamed for or not. And for most it just became something they knew they had to say, but didn't mean. It was done to take the sting out of the offense with an unspoken, "I promise not to do it again". Yeah! That's why being made to say "I'm sorry" never positioned us to take responsibility for what we were rightfully being accused of. And in a matter of time we knew we'd do it again. It's amazing because through all the Garden of Eden turmoil and the lessons that could have been learned we've skillfully mastered the art of "dodging" responsibility for our actions as well. Apologizing has become *"null and void"* because of the insincerity that's hidden behind our "I'm sorry."

The major problem for most is that after being taught or made to say "I'm sorry" the importance of saying "I'm Sorry" and meaning it along with asking for forgiveness was not connected. Although reconciliation is not always possible, the lack of both confessions at the time of the offense from both parties is the reason reconciliation has become so much more difficult. In order for offenders to avoid unnecessary periods of lingering un-forgiveness, "I'M SORRY" jointly acknowledged with "PLEASE FORGIVE ME" should become a practice for the healing process to be intentional. Today some Professional Career Coaches teach that saying 'I'm sorry' is neither popular nor necessary. OH REALLY NOW?

It's God's will that you take ownership of all that belongs to you. So PLEASE…Do not approach the process with the infamous *"If I offended you"* line. Everything you've experienced, brokenness, discomfort and hurt has been managed by the power of Holy Spirit. The same power that has and will give you the ability to get results in all Christ has commanded of you. He alone, by the Will of the Father, provides the power to forgive. The quicker you choose to make 'I'm Sorry,' and 'Please Forgive Me' foundational life lessons, which must be practices daily, those difficult times won't seem as difficult as when you first began. The choice is yours. ONE of the greatest possessions in life God has granted us is the power of 'choice.' The power that causes us to surrender, and allows brokenness to bring about change in our lives. Besides where God has not broken us He will never use us, and you can't fake a breaking either. Because just when you think, 'Okay God, I got it,' 'IT' starts all over again.

The Ministry of Holy Spirit is crucial to your understanding that Love and Forgiveness, Repentance and Remorse hand in hand are essential to learning the power of Repenting of your sins (not 'mistakes') and offenses done against others. It should be your desire to 'reflect' who Christ is IN you. Listen, when we see the N.E. Patriots, the Carolina Panthers, the New Orleans Saints or the Tampa Bay Buccaneer fans in their colors, you and I both know just who and what they represent! Those colors are worn with pride and ownership whether their Team wins or loses. Your commitment and dedication to Christ has to supersede that of natural man when it comes to representing the 'Blood' that was shed for you at Calvary. When people meet you they should be able to discern right-a-way who you REPRESENT. The way you carry yourself, your conversation and convictions, and how you live should tell it all. Joyce Meyers preached on the importance of our allowing God to bring us *through brokenness* and this single line stuck in my spirit like *Gorilla Glue*. She said, "There are no drive-through breakthroughs." Now how profound was that? So I encourage you to hold on and buckle-up because unlike Burger King you can't have it your way and God's way too.

For the non-Believer you must have a healthy perspective on life in order to benefit from your good choices. Stop allowing your thoughts to shape you. Recognize the power of choice that you have been given to 'dwell' on what's right over what's wrong or what's good over evil. Plainly put, begin thinking about what you're thinking.

Keep On Forgiving

Then Peter came to Jesus and asked, "Lord, how many times shall I forgive my brother when he sins against me? Up to seven times?" Jesus answered, "I tell you, not seven times, but seventy-seven times. Matthew 18:21-22 (NIV)

Based on Matthew 18:21-22

FORGIVE ONE ANOTHER!

```
A P T Z U H W J E S N N M H H
A W U K G T K E S X G X Q D X
H T K G T W U S M A N Y I D B
E K A J I B F U B C G E U K G
A F S T I M E S U K O O C U W
M W K W N B O T G P E T E R A
O P E R G R E L P W W O X H T
F A D X B R O T H E R G H X E
K O N A F X S D C R Z L Q W Y
X E R S V Q J L E I L O Z R Q
E Z B G W Q D Q D V O R K P H
E N Z Y I E J P Z L M D J I O
S W U Q H V R S E V E N A C W
W L B Q L L E E I I F W C A C
H U S I N S K T D C F X M T C
```

PETER	ANSWERED	MANY	JESUS
SINS	FORGIVE	HOW	LORD
ASKED	TIMES	BROTHER	SEVEN

NOTES
Instead of being all over the place **be Intentional**

_____

_____

_____

_____

_____

_____

_____

_____

_____

_____

_____

_____

_____

_____

_____

_____

_____

_____

_____

_____

_____

_____

*"Through it all I'm learning to Trust in Jesus, I'm learning to Trust in God." Father I'm
learning that I must be intentional in my love towards you, Jesus and all those around me.*

DISCUSSION DAY SEVEN

FORGIVEN TO FORGIVE

"Regardless of the cynicism or ridicule we face, God calls us to His standard of obedience and righteousness. **Dr. Michael Youssef**

Do not be conformed to this world, but be transformed by the renewal of your mind, that by testing you may discern what is the will of God, what is good and acceptable and perfect. **Romans 12:2 (ESV**

WE ARE FREE!

WILLINGNESS IS THE KEY

Well, you're one Discussion Day away from the end of your journey. I pray that if you are a Believer by this point you've learned the importance of being 'willing' to obediently submit unconditionally while allowing God by Holy Spirit to get you where He Wills for you to be. As vessels of Christ we must live life by what makes us different from the world. We are being sanctified as Vessels of Truth, and the truth of God's Word is His Love.

If you started this journey as a non-believer an invitation is being extended to you to receive Christ Jesus as your personal Savior and ultimate Lord. Over and over it's been declared that only by Faith in him can real forgiveness be extended and received. If you're working through this journey in a group and you're sincerely ready to acknowledge that you are a sinner and ready to surrender by repenting and taking the step of Faith, ask the Group Leader to stop and guide you to the Throne of Grace. God who has the wonderful plan of Salvation is extending an invitation to you right here, right now. He'll not only become your Savior and Lord, but Friend. The Bible says in Romans 10:9-11 that, *9"If you declare with your mouth, "Jesus is Lord," and believe in your heart that God raised him from the dead, you will be saved. 10 For it is with you heart that you believe and are justified, and it is with your mouth that you profess your faith and are saved, 11As scripture says, "Anyone who believes in him will never be put to shame."* It is by His Grace (undeserved favor) that we are saved, not by anything we can or will do, it is a gift of God to us through Faith in His son. Believing and Confessing Who Christ is and what he did at Calvary just for you is the start. To *successfully finish* this life journey absolute surrender to the Lordship of Christ through your obedience to His Word is a must. Author Andrew Murray concurred in a quote when he wrote: *"The only condition for obtaining God's full blessing is **absolute surrender** to Him."* My prayer is that as you develop a lifestyle of obedience you'll begin to witness the power and wonders of living a life of faith and forgiveness IN him each day, moment by moment under his Lordship.

All across this country we've suffered major power outages but know this, the Sovereign, All Mighty God has infinite power. He's a big enough God to handle all your cares. In 1 Peter 5:7 we're given permission to 'cast' every one of our cares on Him. I encourage you to stay away from using human wisdom and reasoning. Live an authentic Christian life by keeping Christ First, reverencing Him, and taking him very seriously. Abide in Him by drawing life from The Word, which is our Final Authority. In your prayer time ask God for His divine wisdom without doubting and your faith IN Christ will begin to grow. If you've made a decision to follow Him, WELCOME to the Family of God! You have been **"FORGIVEN TO FORGIVE!"**

THE WHITE FLAG

I Finally Forgave My Ex-husband

Growing up I loved watching war movies. They became my favorite over comedy, scary, or suspense; you name it, they were the bomb. Literally! After I was born-again the Lord showed me a spiritual principle at work that I caught onto. He took me back to the scene where after a fierce battle the American troops took the enemy captive. The truth was demonstrated in the very part of the movie I loved most. When the enemy gave-up, they would take dirty white rags, tie them to the tips of their weapons, throw them in the air and surrender to the Americans. I would get so excited and emotional that I would jump up crying and yell, *"That's right, step back Jack!"* It was at that point the battle was over! What I gleaned was that the very same position the enemy troop took, I had to take. Total surrender! That was what God required of me.

Jesus yielded himself and became subject to the Will of his Father on that cross, so then those of us who declare to be His must be willing to yield ourselves as well. Because God is after your spiritual growth, as you surrender to Christ, over time you will become more and more like Him. Initially, you might battle with being quick with the mouth; you might struggle with an attitude and with things that have become habitual. There may even be tendencies to experience fits of carnality. And you may even struggle with coming under godly authority. But as you begin to yield to God's Word your new position IN Christ Jesus will bring old practices under the transforming influence and sanctifying power of Holy Spirit. If allowed, He will break every yoke of bondage and soften your stubborn heart filling it with what Galatians 5:22-23 (NIV) declares to be the fruit of the Spirit. Love, joy, peace, longsuffering, kindness, goodness, faithfulness, gentleness, and self-control all of which are the evidences of one living IN Christ Jesus.

One Sunday morning following Worship Service I finally threw up 'my white flag' and released my Ex off the tip of the *un-forgiveness hook* I'd dangled him from for years. Right then, right there I repented for my attitude towards him, which was not Christ like or pleasing to God. The Emotional toll being paid came to an end. By finally laying and leaving it at the foot of the Cross I accepted the truth with where the battle actually laid. Taking personal ownership and confessing that I was really angry with myself all along for being so stupid was huge! Blaming my Ex for everything had become a habit, but right then it ended. Total deliverance came as I earnestly began praying and asking God to save him. At that moment I went from being mad with me to being more intimate with God. The issues I had with him were hardly ever the issue; I just had a gigantic 'chip' on my shoulder and refused to flick it off. Becoming scripturally dead to my carnal way of thinking required my putting on the 'Whole' Armor of God, especially the Helmet. I was being processed through 'The Blood' to Breakthrough while learning that unilateral forgiveness releases the other person without them asking to be forgiven.

That evening I sat down and intentionally wrote him a letter. It ended up being three sheets of legal size paper back-to-back long. When it was all said and done the letter was never about him, but about me. I quit posturing, sat in that 'still place' and took what was defined in the teaching I received as, a realistic appraisal of the sin done against me. So, I apologized and asked for forgiveness. The moment I dropped that letter in the mailbox I was free and I no longer felt paralyzed emotionally, circumstantially or spiritually. The hurt associated with just the thought of him, our marriage or the mentioning of his name was gone. The decision to no longer use him as an excuse for all my bad choices was over. No longer did I have to feel bound by the hurt of my past. I began intentionally experiencing the Freedom that came with Forgiveness.

In all that you learn in relationship with Christ, THE most important take-a-way is your ability to **totally trust, obey and rely on God and on Him alone**. Gradually you will begin to develop stability, maturity, compassion, clarity, and humility. All the characteristics successfully gained through your journey to a productive, loving relationship with the Savior and each other. No matter how educated, well off or Titled you are never trust in your limited knowledge and understanding, or others opinions, only on His Word.

Please hear me and hear me clearly my friends, you will be required many more times to extend that same forgiveness in many, many different situations.

"If we begin to get a glimpse of the vast glory of God, we will realize that many of our conflicts are like two ants arguing about which is taller while standing in front of Mount Everest." **Pastor Chris Brauns (Unpacking Forgiveness)**

DISCUSSION TIME

SHARE YOUR THOUGHTS ON THE FOLLOWING QUOTES

'If your goal is to win the fight then you have already lost.

Reconciliation is the true victory!'

-Jen Smith

Forgive, not because they deserve forgiveness, but because you deserve peace.

(Author Unknown)

"Love your enemies, do good to those who hate you, bless those who curse you, pray for those who mistreat you."

Luke 6:27-28

'FORGIVENESS

IS ME GIVING UP MY RIGHT TO HURT YOU FOR HURTING ME'

Qfor quotes

"To forgive is to set a prisoner free and discover that the prisoner was you."

Lewis B. Smedes

"LIFE BECOMES EASIER WHEN YOU LEARN TO ACCEPT AN APOLOGY YOU NEVER GOT." **Robert Brault**

THANK YOU for sacrificing and investing the time, transparency and willingness to working through to FREEDOM. Let's take a look back and **REVIEW** each step taken so far. Freely share your thoughts, concerns, challenges and suggestions with each another.

Discussion Day#1 "We Must ID the 'Root'" Share just how DIFFICULT it really was for you to take that **1st step and admit the root(s) of your un-forgiveness battle.**

LIST ALL THE GOOD, BAD AND UGLY TIMES.

_____

_____

_____

Discussion Day #2 "Forgiveness Doesn't Come Cheap." Share how CHALLENGING it was to accept the fact that Christ's love for you didn't come cheap, and now you were being required by God to extend that same 'love cost' to others. **How did that initially sit with you?**

LIST WHY IT'S IMPORTANT THAT WE KNOW, ACCEPT AND LIVE THIS TRUTH.

_____

_____

_____

Discussion Day #3 "What Did I Do?" How DIFFICULT was it to look back, examine yourself, **and then accept responsibility for extending forgiveness to someone who offended you?**

WHAT WAS THE MOST DIFFICULT THING FOR YOU TO DO?

_____

_____

_____

Discussion Day #4 "It's Not Easy to Forgive Those Who Offended Me!" What were your biggest BATTLES, **and most important takeaways with breaking free of this mindset?**

HAVE YOU RECOGNIZED THAT THIS IS A LIFETIME COMMITMENT?

_____

_____

_____

Discussion Day #5 "Why is God so Bent On My Forgiving Others?" Thinking back, what "aha" moments did you experience GRAPPLING with this question? **How well are you doing right now?**

SHARE YOUR THOUGHTS

_____

_____

_____

Discussion Day #6 "INTENTIONAL" Whether you are the offended or the offender, how important has becoming 'Intentional'" (in your actions and responses) been to your being able to forgive and/or reconcile your situation,

HOW HAS GETTING FREE OF ALL THAT WEIGHT HELPED YOU?

_____

_____

_____

Discussion Day #7 "Forgiven to Forgive" How important has SURRENDER become to you, as a believer or non-believer, in understanding that your willingness to obey the Biblical Principles of God, no matter the circumstance **will lead to victory?**

Share

_____

_____

_____

DISCUSSION DAY EIGHT

HOW DO I MOVE FROM FORGIVENESS TO RECONCILIATION?

Reconciliation means to 'change' or 'exchange.' So Reconciliation involves change in the relationships between God and man, and exchange between man and man.

"All this is from God, who through Christ reconciled us to himself and gave us the ministry of reconciliation; that is, in Christ God was reconciling the world to himself, not counting their trespasses against them, and entrusting to us the message of reconciliation".
II Corinthians 5: 18-19

THE REAL CHALLENGE FOR THE OFFENDER

With my Ex-husband I intentionally dragged my feet hesitating to forgive him simply because I thought it automatically meant I'd be pardoning him of any responsibility whatsoever. But through my studies and understanding of the teachings on the subject of Forgiveness Vs Reconciliation I found they were two separate practices, and neither does one necessarily lead to the other. Nearly three years after writing him and asking for his forgiveness my children and I moved back to Boston. One day I received a call asking 'me' for forgiveness and letting me know that he always loved me, and was glad I was his children's mother. That had to be a real challenge for him. But because of my willingness to submit to the Will of God by Faith and knowing my heart was clean towards him I simply replied with a, 'thank you.' At that very moment we were reconciled. Pastor Rod Hembree made this thought provoking statement; "the reality of faith is hard to understand. Yet, it is simple. Many want their faith written out, so they can see what they are supposed to be or do. But God is a Living Person Who is perfect. When we serve the Lord Jesus Christ, we serve the Living LORD. At times, we must make tough decisions about our actions. We need real faith in Christ to do that. We must trust in God."

HOW DO I MOVE FROM FORGIVENESS TO RECONCILIATION?

Reconciliation Finally Came!

Two years after my dad's death I began feeling detached from my Home Church and didn't quite understand why, but sensed God was calling me out of Boston. After receiving confirmation and counsel from a Wise Man of God, in March of 2005, I left relocating to Virginia Beach with my son and his family. Leaving behind my family, church family and close friends I followed the leading of Holy Spirit for my life. The Ministry I joined actively provided me a place of Worship and continued spiritual growth. Once while visiting us my mother loved VA and our pastor so much that to our surprise she decided to move from Boston as well. So in 2007 ma relocated to Virginia Beach. I've got to confess that her stay was very celebratory, encouraging and enlightening for me. Ma bought back to my memory family history facts and legacy stories my siblings and I grew up hearing and witnessing. That became very important as I was in the beginning stages of writing "All Through The Blood-Forgiven to Forgive." Believe it or not my mother and I actually enjoyed being in each other's company. It was fantastic. Un-expectantly though before the end of that year she expressed an urgent need to return to Boston, so my son and I made preparations for ma to head home.

The day my mother boarded that plane will forever be embedded in my memory like it was yesterday. I really hated seeing her leave. Within weeks of returning to Boston she fell ill. Ultimately she endured emergency surgery followed by a rehab stay. At one point I was unable to speak directly with her, which troubled me, but I kept in touch through her nurses, or whoever was visiting with her at the time. I made sure to tell them to let her know that the book was coming along fine.

One morning my mother weighed heavily on my heart and I discerned that something was terribly wrong. When I got to work there was an urgent email telling me she had been constantly asking for me and that I should get in touch with her right away. I thought "mmm, if my mother is asking for 'me' something has got to be wrong." But I knew deep in my heart it was important that I make contact ASAP. All I needed was to hear her voice in order to tell how she was really doing. So I called the facility where she was staying. The rehab nurse was kind enough to bring ma to the nurse's station so we could talk. The moment I heard her voice I knew something was terribly wrong. When my mother realized it was me on the phone, in a strained whisper she asked, "Marian is that you?" I replied, "Yes Ma, it's me! How are you?" Not even answering my question, she quickly proceeded to tell me, "*Marian, I love 'all' my children.*" Before I had a chance to respond she repeated it again as though she wanted to be sure I heard what she was saying. "Marian, *I love 'all' my children.*" What I was hearing for the first time in my life was that my mother 'loved me'. Such peace flowed over me that I began to cry and said, "Ma, I love you too!" In a split second what Jesus told me as a child, that she didn't know how to love me, came to mind. Her statement clearly demonstrated that her inability to show me the love I desperately needed did not mean that deep in her heart she didn't *love me*. The validation I waited for all my life, as indirect as it was said, came right then. That was her time and way of reconciling years had between us. Reconciliation finally came. Pastor Chris Brauns offers spiritual wisdom in his book "Unpacking Forgiveness*"* when he clearly distinguishes between a kind of therapeutic forgiveness that may make us feel better, and a genuine forgiveness that actually brings about reconciliation. Through my process of forgiving her it only took me to forgive, but to be able to reconcile it took the both of us. So my mother and I were genuinely reconciled. That was on Monday, March 17, 2008 and on Resurrection Sunday, March 23rd ma went home to be with the Lord.

God's heart is that we be reconciled one with another, but take notice please; this isn't always possible if the offender is not willing. And because they aren't the same, we will take the time necessary to move through the process very carefully during this discussion. For those who have willfully offended others, the burden of this process falls totally on you. The success of any act of reconciliation depends totally on the attitude of the offender towards the one offended. To those who have been abused physically, mentally or psychologically taken advantage of…the burden of this process is OFF YOU.

Growing up we were made to say "I'm sorry" with no real sense of being sorry whatsoever and unwilling to guarantee it wouldn't happen again, but this is not one of those moments. Real reconciliation has definite steps and signs of open communication and remorse.

Whether you are a Believer or not, the next steps will either make or break you in this Forgiveness process. **The Challenge will begin NOW!**

TO THE OFFENDER

THERE ARE NECESSARY STEPS TO RECONCILIATION:

In order to accomplish the following you must be very intentional in taking the required steps necessary in accomplishing real reconciliation. These are representative of *Genuine Repentance* that must be displayed on your behalf or there will be no real reconciliation. Let's go through and discuss them as we move forward. **Ready?**

It is important that you be 'WILLING' to DO the following

1. Take full responsibility **(your actions must be truthful. So don't lie)**

2. Welcome Accountability **(people who will not hold back any punches and are not afraid to hold you to task should be included in your process)**

3. Write out a plan of approach **(share this with your accountability team)**

4. discontinue the offensive behavior **(you were wrong, so admit it)**

5. Don't come off defensively **(defensiveness reveals an un-repentant heart)**

6. do Not downplay your behavior **(even if it wasn't intentional an offense happened, own up to it)**

7. Please do not fake your sincerity **(if the offended detects or questions your sincerity, the process could come to a halt)**

8. Make restitution where necessary **(if need be, be prepared)**

Your role as the offender in the reconciliation process is serious and must be taken VERY SERIOUSLY. If the offended refuses to hear, accept or acknowledge your attempt to make things right, there will be **no reconciliation**. REMEMBER IT TAKES **TWO** TO RECONCILE.

WARNING TO THE OFFENDED

- Do not attempt to control or manipulate the circumstances now that the burden is on the other person to reconcile. You do not have permission to retaliate. For the Ladies on this journey, you know just what I'm talking about. A proper attitude is equally as important for Peace to come. If not it will be like 'microwaving your offenders sins' for breakfast. Former President Ronald Reagan said it best, "Peace is not the absence of conflict; it is the ability to handle conflict by peaceable means." You be the better person. If you begin having a tough time accepting your offenders attempt to restore a peaceable relationship "Flip the Script" and remember God used that offense for your good. Your offender has been used in the hand of God to mature you and for His Glory.

- Remember with God's Grace and help, you have the power in Holy Spirit needed to reconcile with 'anyone' over 'anything.' The process will only be as complicated as you make it. So in order to gain the victory 'you' may be required to display enormous restraint. If the process doesn't look like it's going well you remain persistent and determined to get through the necessary stages, **No matter what!** Speedy solutions aren't always possible. So please be patient.

- Reconciliation may involve several other folk around you. Depending on the agreed upon guidelines between you and the offender the process may take a while. It will not only take God's help but the strength of 'your' will, of 'your 'heart, and soul to undertake the process. It could get chaotic but again you be the better person. For extra support keep close family members close, and close friends even closer. They will provide the support; back-up and encouragement when needed, and may even have to throw a challenge or two in order to keep you on track. **Back-up is a necessity!** When the apology for the offense has been made and you discern genuine repentance has been demonstrated, do not become arrogant. Instead offer your hand of forgiveness. If both of you are not on board reconciliation will not happen.

- For your willingness to listen to and hear your offender out God may require a level of compassion on your part towards him or her that you've never experienced or ever thought about granting. This may or may not be easy, BUT GOD! Be Prepared.

- Under no circumstances or for any reason are you to throw any part of what was done to you back in the face of your offender. Once forgiveness has been extended and real healing begins the thoughts you once pondered will no longer be accompanied by the '*sting*' and 'bruising' that went along with the hurt. Understand that being reconciled does not mean you have to make lunch or dinner dates to prove anything. You do not have to become BFF"s again! That could happen but it's not required for the process to be complete. One of the benefits of your reconciled relationship is that memories of past hurt, all your undealt with issues, the what, whys and how-comes will begin to be healed. You'll even start looking at your offender differently. You are now an official Reconciliation Ambassador on behalf of Christ, and can now begin moving forward in freedom, freedom that you hadn't experienced in a long time.

A NONNEGOTIABLE CHECKLIST FOR THE OFFENDED

If a scheduled meeting time has been set but it's not convenient
or doesn't feel right to you, do the following:

If approached to begin the reconciliation process and you're not ready, make it clear to your offender why you'd rather wait. You'll make no greater mistake than to begin a challenge when you aren't prepared emotionally to handle it. If the desire is authentic on the part of the offender he or she will understand and will be willing to 'wait.' Do not allow the process to go beyond an agreed upon amount of time made between both parties.

Make sure your intentions and motives are pure in God's sight before allowing the process to begin. The scripture says that GOD ALONE SEARCHES THE HEART and examines the mind. Before you make a move be sure that you've examined yourself prior to coming before your offender and that the forgiveness you extended to start this process is 'authentic.' A harsh or mean demeanor or bad attitude will stop everything. Do not retaliate. You could have annihilated your offender, but instead you chose to do this God's way and forgive. When the process begins both parties together should make sure boundaries are set. Limits and clear guidelines for accountability and restoration needed to be in place assuring that no one steps out of bounds. Respect yourself. And be sure your expectations of the offender are realistic.

Please walk in humility. This process can't be for show. It must be from the heart minus pride. When we are prideful, arrogance causes us to walk independent of God, and He hates it. If you begin to think more highly of yourself the whole process will fall apart. God will not be Honored and you'll end-up back at square one. Be sure to earnestly pray for your offender prior to the meeting. God commands that you pray for those who have despitefully used you, and who have said all manner of evil about you. And that's non-negotiable. He allows for NO exceptions.

If this applies, please take responsibility. Be willing to confess whatever involvement you may have had in causing the offense. Confession before God is a must first and it breaks down any defensive barriers that may have been built between you and your offender. Plus it puts you in the position again of being 'the better person.' And when the opportunity arises with the right attitude be honest and upfront with your offender about how you were personally affected by them. A detailed extended list is not necessary. A quick summary of what you experienced would be beneficial for him or her to hear while computing the severity of their offense.

Keep the spiritual eyes of your understanding of God's Word open and you'll quickly discern any attempt the enemy might make to derail the reconciliation process. Remember 'God Is In Control' and that this whole process is for your spiritual growth and His Honor and Glory!

If you've honestly worked through each step and your hearts pure before God then contact your offender, your 'accountability team' (if needed) and get the process started. **BE BLESSED, and remember…God is in Control!**

SCRIPTURES OF ENCOURAGEMENT IN TIMES OF NEED

"Father, Thank You because through this entire process Your Word has proven to me that You are my Way Maker, Miracle Worker, Promise Keeper and Light in the Darkness."

Psalms 34:17-20 (ESV) [17] When the righteous cry for help, the LORD hears and delivers them out of all their troubles. [18] The LORD is near to the brokenhearted and saves the crushed in spirit.

I Peter 5:10 (ESV) [10] **And after you have suffered a little while, the God of all grace, who has called you to his eternal glory in Christ, will himself restore, confirm, strengthen, and establish you..**

Exodus 14:14 (ESV) [14] The LORD WILL FIGHT FOR YOU, AND YOU HAVE ONLY TO BE SILENT."

2 Corinthians 12:9 (NIV) [9] But he said to me, "My grace is sufficient for you, for my power is made perfect in weakness." Therefore I will boast all the more gladly about my weaknesses, so that Christ's power may rest on me.

Psalm 51:10 (NIV) [10] Create in me a pure heart, O God, and renew a right spirit within me.

James 5:16 (NIV) [16] Therefore confess your sins to each other and pray for each other so that you may be healed. The prayer of a righteous person is powerful and effective.

Jeremiah 29:11 (NIV) [11] For I know the plans I have for you," declares the LORD, "PLANS TO PROSPER YOU AND NOT TO HARM YOU, PLANS TO GIVE YOU HOPE AND A FUTURE.

2 Chronicles 7:14 (NIV) [14] If my people who are called by my name will humble themselves and pray, and seek my face and turn from their wicked ways, then I will hear from heaven and I will forgive their sin and heal their land.

Ephesians 3:20 (NIV) [20] Now unto him who is able to do immeasurably more than we ask or imagine, according to his power that is at work within us, to him be glory in the church and In Christ Jesus throughout all generations, for ever and ever! Amen

Isaiah 54:17 (NIV)

[17] no weapon forged against you will prevail, and you will refute every tongue that accuses you. This is the heritage of the servants of the LORD, and this is their vindication from me," declares the LORD.

CONGRATULATIONS!!!

....You have successfully completed what is actually the beginning of a life-long committed process. When you find yourself looking back...press forward applying all that you've learned.

Following is a '**Certificate of Completion**' that's being presented in Honor of the time you've invested to successfully going through to the end of this Discussion Guide, and for your willingness to be challenged along the way to **Complete Forgiveness**.

If you are part of a Discussion Group kindly have your Group Leader sign the Certificate.

Marian E. Turenne, Author

May The Lord bless you and keep you; The Lord make his face shine upon you, and be gracious to you; The Lord lift up his countenance upon you, and give you peace. **Numbers 6:24-26 (NKJV)**

MOVING FORWARD

Romans 12:1-2 (MSG)

[1-2] So here's what I want you to do, God helping you: Take your everyday, ordinary life – your sleeping, eating, going-to-work, and walking-around life- and place it before God as an offering. Embracing what God does for you is the best thing you can do for him. Don't become as well-adjusted to your culture that you fit into it without even thinking. Instead, fix your attention on God. You'll be changed from the inside out. Readily recognize what he wants from you, and quickly respond to it. Unlike the culture around you, who is always dragging you down to its level of immaturity, God brings the best out of you. He develops well-formed maturity in you.

CERTIFICATE OF COMPLETION

This acknowledges that

_____

Has successfully completed

The 'FORGIVEN TO FORGIVE'

DISCUSSION GUIDE CHALLENGE

Presented By
Marian E. Turenne, author

"To forgive is the highest most beautiful form of Love. In return, you will receive untold Peace and Happiness." Robert Mull

_____   _____
Date of Completion   Group Leader's Signature

Printed in the United States
By Bookmasters